Native Peoples of THE SOUTHWEST

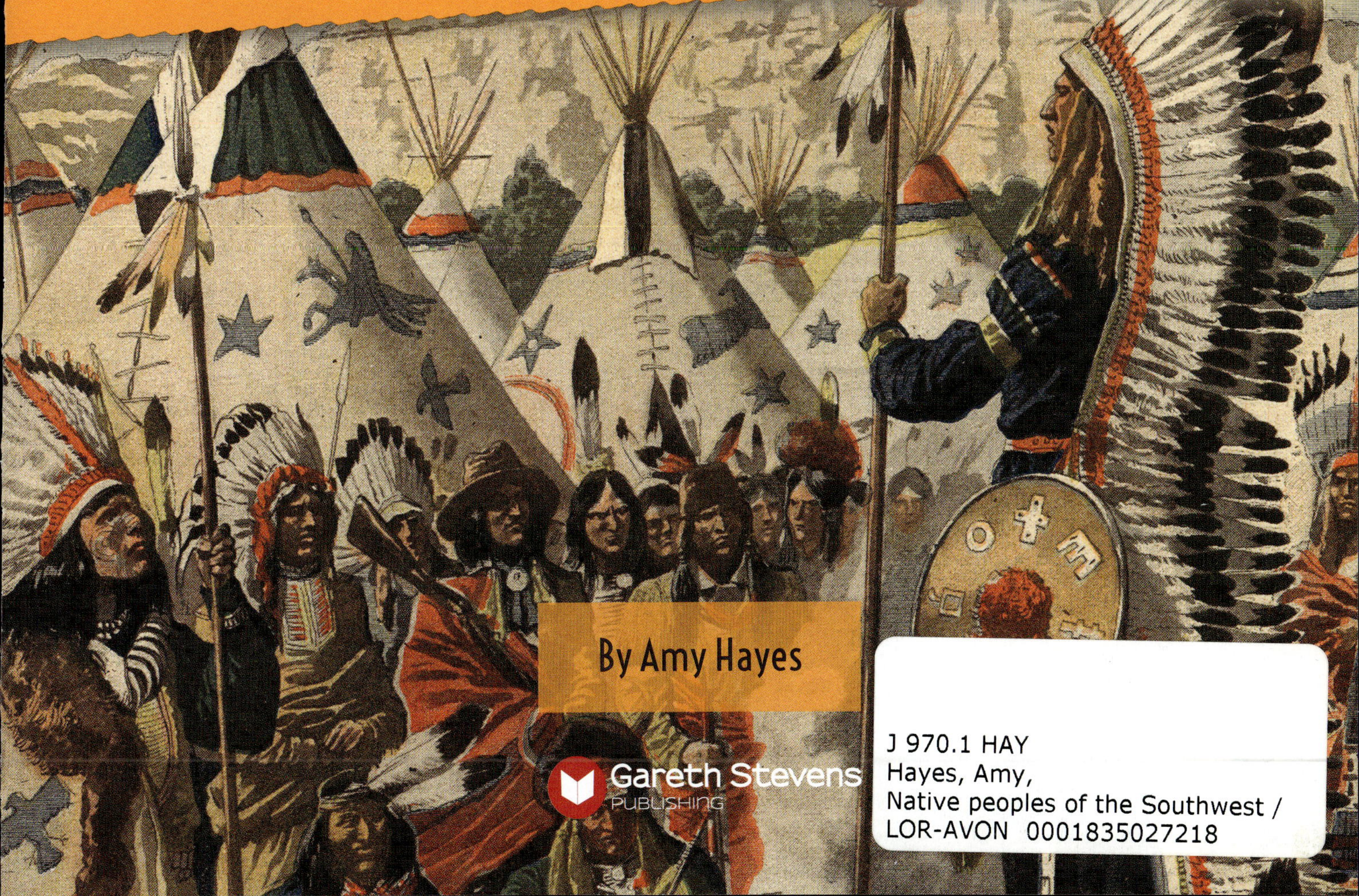

By Amy Hayes

Gareth Stevens
PUBLISHING

Please visit our website, www.garethstevens.com. For a free color catalog of all our high-quality books, call toll free 1-800-542-2595 or fax 1-877-542-2596.

Library of Congress Cataloging-in-Publication Data

Names: Hayes, Amy, author.
Title: Native peoples of the Southwest / Amy Hayes.
Description: New York : Gareth Stevens Publishing, 2016. | Series: Native peoples of North America | Includes index.
Identifiers: LCCN 2016000323 | ISBN 9781482448351 (pbk.) | ISBN 9781482448207 (library bound) | ISBN 9781482447668 (6 pack)
Subjects: LCSH: Indians of North America–Southwest, New–Juvenile literature.
Classification: LCC E78.S7 H396 2016 | DDC 979.004/97–dc23
LC record available at http://lccn.loc.gov/2016000323

First Edition

Published in 2017 by
Gareth Stevens Publishing
111 East 14th Street, Suite 349
New York, NY 10003

Copyright © 2017 Gareth Stevens Publishing

Designer: Samantha DeMartin
Editor: Kristen Nelson

Photo credits: Series art AlexTanya/Shutterstock.com; cover, p. 1 Leemage/Universal Images Group/Getty Images; p. 5 Steve Bower/Shutterstock.com; p. 7 (map) AlexCovarrubias/Wikimedia Commons; p. 7 (main) Australian Camera/Shutterstock.com; p. 9 WorldPictures/Shutterstock.com; p. 11 Fæ/Wikimedia Commons; p. 13 MIKE NELSON/AFP/Getty Images; pp. 15, 17 Buyenlarge/Archive Photos/Getty Images; p. 19 (main) Michael Ochs Archives/Michael Ochs Archives/Getty Images; p. 19 (turquoise) Alexander Hoffmann/Shutterstock.com; p. 21 Peter V. Bianchi/National Geographic/Getty Images; p. 23 ivanastar/E+/Getty Images; p. 25 Hulton Archive/Archive Photos/Getty Images; p. 27 Soerfm/Wikimedia Commons.

All rights reserved. No part of this book may be reproduced in any form without permission in writing from the publisher, except by a reviewer.

Printed in the United States of America

CPSIA compliance information: Batch #CS16GS: For further information contact Gareth Stevens, New York, New York at 1-800-542-2595.

CONTENTS

A Stunning Reminder 4
Where They Lived 6
Settling Down 8
Religious Beliefs 10
Governed by Family 12
Men and Women 14
Homes and Settlements 16
Useful and Beautiful 18
The Many Pueblo Indians 20
Who Were the Hopi? 22
Apache Hunters 24
Geronimo: An Apache Hero 26
Native Peoples of the Southwest Today 28
Glossary 30
For More Information 31
Index 32

Words in the glossary appear in **bold** type the first time they are used in the text.

A Stunning REMINDER

The sun beats down on Mesa Verde National Park. The air is hot and dry. At the bottom of a cliff stands a large group of ancient buildings. These buildings make up an old village today called Cliff Palace. Though it can be quite hot in this part of Colorado, inside the buildings, the air is nice and cool.

These buildings, located in southwest Colorado, are just one reminder of the history and **culture** of the native peoples of the North American Southwest.

When it was in use, Cliff Palace had around 150 rooms.

Where They LIVED

The first people living in the southwestern part of North America arrived as early as 9000 BC. They lived where they could hunt and gather food, and many moved from place to place. Today, the areas where these people lived are parts of the states of Colorado, Utah, Nevada, New Mexico, and Texas, in addition to northern Mexico.

Much of this land is hot and **arid**. Even though it's very dry, most of the soil is good for farming.

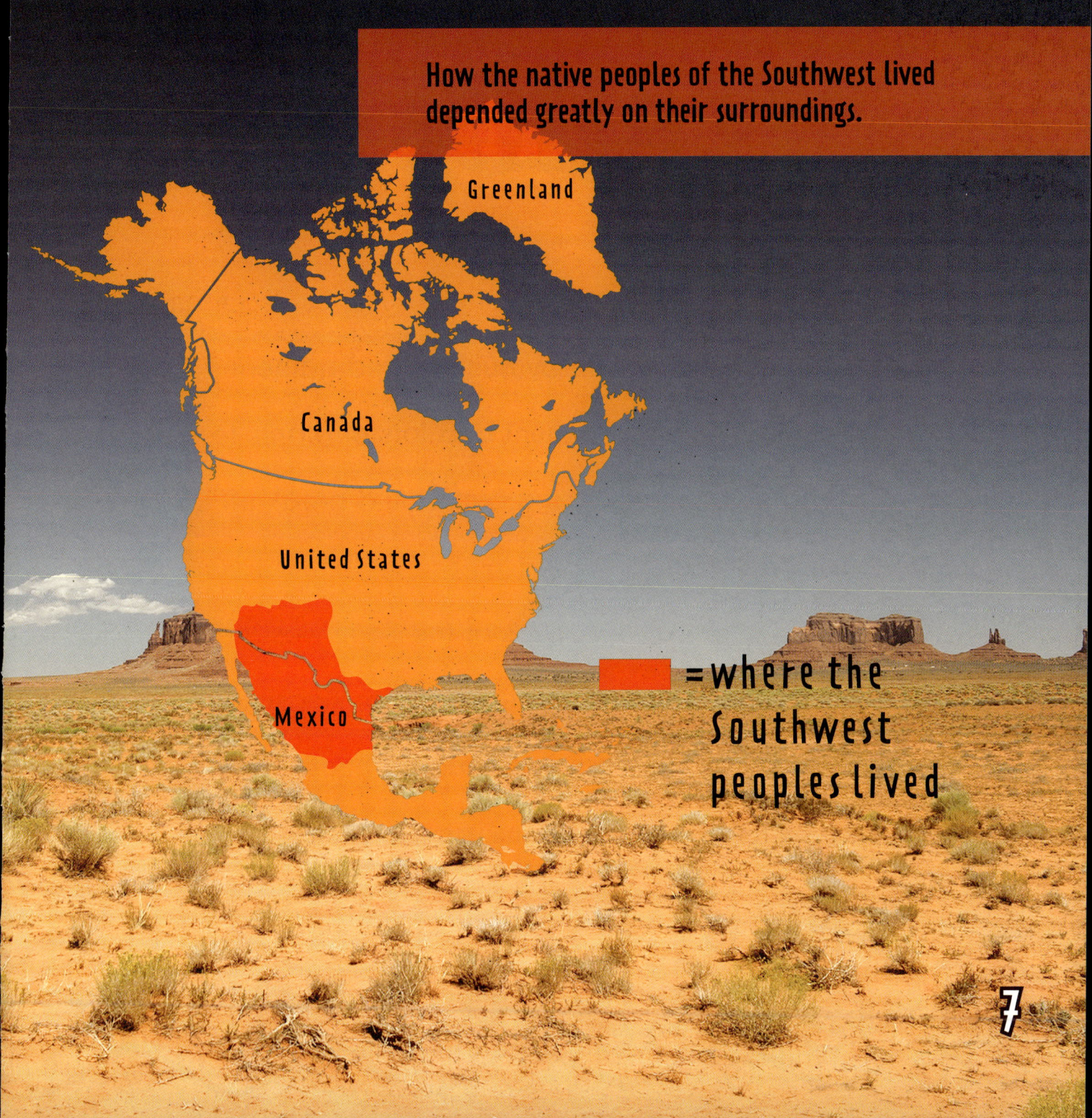

Settling DOWN

Many of the early peoples of the Southwest, such as the Cochise Culture, survived by hunting and gathering. There were many animals to hunt and lots of plants to eat. If food became hard to find, a group would break off and move to a new place.

By 200 BC, the native groups of the Southwest had begun to farm. The **Ancestral** Puebloans (or Anasazi), Mogollon, and Hohokam built **permanent** homes and grew crops such as maize (corn), beans, and squash.

The Ancestral Pueblo culture was found in the Southwest from about AD 100 to 1600. The **descendants** of this native group are the modern Pueblo. The Ancestral Puebloans lived in cliff dwellings, or homes, like the one in this photograph.

TELL ME MORE

For many years, the native peoples of the Southwest raised turkeys and dogs. When the Spanish arrived, they brought sheep, horses, and donkeys. Native groups quickly learned how to raise these animals, too.

Religious BELIEFS

Religion was an important part of the native cultures of the Southwest. Each group had its own beliefs, gods, and **traditions**. These religions were closely tied to the natural world.

The Apache believed powerful forces, such as mountains and animals, controlled the world. These forces were sung to and talked to often so they would be kind to the Apache. Other groups, such as some of the Ancestral Puebloans, believed even the tiniest ant affected the **universe**.

The Apache have an important ceremony that welcomes young girls into womanhood.

TELL ME MORE

The Ancestral Puebloans held **ceremonies** to help the rain fall and the crops grow. Many believed the world would end if traditions like these weren't followed.

Governed by FAMILY

The native peoples of the Southwest commonly lived and worked as families. The oldest man in a household was the head of the family and made decisions. Families that worked together were called bands. If a decision needed to be made, the heads of all families would come together and discuss it. When many bands joined together, they were called a tribe.

Beyond family and **councils** made up of the heads of different bands, most peoples of the Southwest didn't have set governments.

Councils of Native Americans still meet today. Al Gore met with the All Indian Pueblo Council during 2000 when he was running for president.

TELL ME MORE

The Zuni and Hopi were matrilineal, meaning that the man moved into the woman's house after marriage. In these societies, women were the head of the household, though men still met on councils.

Men and WOMEN

Like many other native cultures of the Southwest, men and women of the Zuni people often worked together. For example, men built the houses, and women strengthened the outside walls.

The men were in charge of religious ceremonies, and some became priests. Men also became warriors, or fighters, and fought for their village's safety. Women were in charge of raising animals, crops, and children. They made sure everyone had enough to eat and took care of their houses.

Only Zuni women could make pottery. Zuni men made other kinds of art.

TELL ME MORE

The Zuni lived mostly along the Rio Grande and the Colorado River.

Homes and SETTLEMENTS

Many native groups in the Southwest started out as nomadic, which means they moved from place to place. The Apache built small houses made of brush and dried plants. These were called wikiups. They were easy to build and move when the Apache went to a new area.

The Navajo created more permanent homes called hogans. Hogans were built with tree bark, mud, grass, and wood. The Ancestral Puebloans built houses out of adobe, clay that was baked in the sun until it was hard.

Adobe homes could be several stories high. People climbed ladders to get from floor to floor.

Useful and BEAUTIFUL

Brightly colored cloth, pots, and **jewelry** were all created by native peoples of the Southwest. The Apache were known for making beautiful jewelry pieces out of silver and pretty stones like jade. The Hopi and Zuni are praised for the **designs** that covered their pots.

The Ancestral Puebloans had a long tradition of **weaving**. Then, once their descendants, the Pueblo, started growing cotton, weaving became a popular art. Clothing and blankets could include many colors and pretty designs. Everything the peoples of the Southwest made had a purpose in addition to being beautiful.

This photograph shows the traditional clothing the Zuni wear for special occasions.

TELL ME MORE

Even the jewelry Southwest cultures wore had a purpose. Turquoise was a special bluish-green stone that was worn to bring happiness and good health.

The Many PUEBLO INDIANS

The term "Pueblo Indians" doesn't mean one certain group of native peoples, but many different groups. They're all called Pueblo Indians because of the settlements of adobe houses, or pueblos, they lived in. Some well-known groups of Pueblo peoples are the Zuni, Keres, and Jemez.

A pueblo was made up of many buildings that were connected, somewhat like an apartment building. Each pueblo was an independent community with its own leaders. A family would live in one or two rooms of the pueblo.

TELL ME MORE

"Pueblo" is the Spanish word for village.

A pueblo had a special room for religious ceremonies called a kiva. It was built underground, and when a person entered a kiva, they were said to walk into the underworld.

Who Were the HOPI?

The Hopi were another group of Pueblo Indians. They lived in an area called Black Mesa in northern Arizona. The Hopi, like other Pueblo Indians, were farmers. They grew many kinds of corn, as well as squash, cotton, and tobacco.

Religion played a huge part in Hopi society. The leader of a Hopi group was also its priest. An important religious tradition they had was the kachina doll. These handmade wooden dolls each stand for a kachina, or kind spirit, that visited where the Hopi lived.

Kachina dolls are made out of the root of the cottonwood tree.

TELL ME MORE

"Hopi" means "peaceful person."

23

Apache HUNTERS

The Apache were a nomadic group originally from Canada. They likely came to the Southwest around AD 1100, later living as far south as the Rio Grande.

The Apache were skilled warriors who were known for riding horses well. In fact, the Apache may have been the first Native Americans to ride horses when the Spanish brought them to North America. The Apache hunted bison for meat and clothing. They also traded with Pueblo villages as they moved around the Southwest.

The Apache greatly depended on horses for travel, war, and hunting.

25

Geronimo: AN APACHE HERO

European explorers had called North America the New World, overlooking the native peoples who had lived there for thousands of years. By the late 1800s, the United States had taken over much of the Southwest, and native groups lost their traditional homelands.

Geronimo was an Apache who was angry his home had been taken away. For many years, he fought US forces that wanted Apache land. Geronimo became a hero to his people and many others in the Southwest.

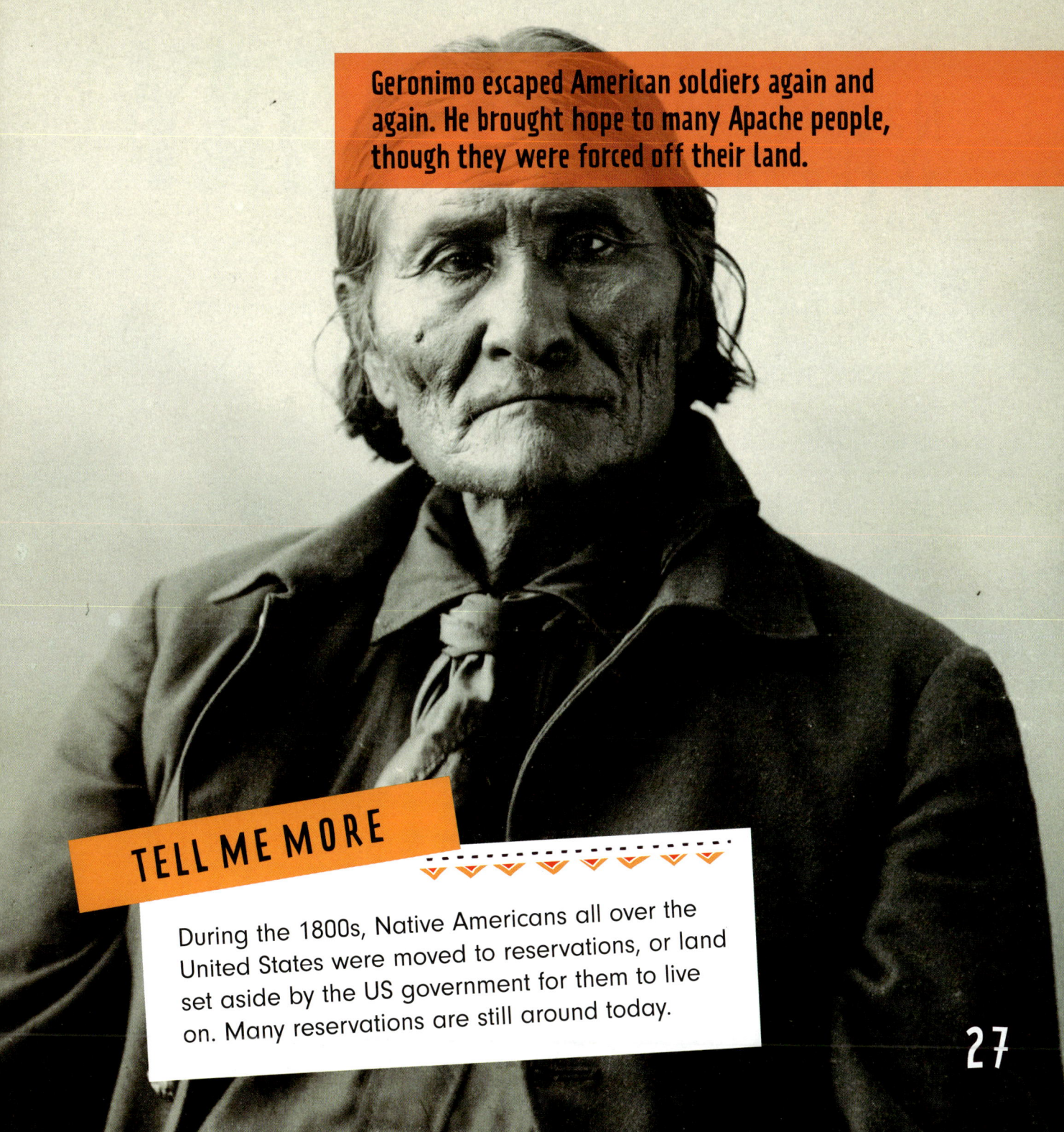

Geronimo escaped American soldiers again and again. He brought hope to many Apache people, though they were forced off their land.

TELL ME MORE

During the 1800s, Native Americans all over the United States were moved to reservations, or land set aside by the US government for them to live on. Many reservations are still around today.

Native Peoples of the Southwest TODAY

Southwest Indians have dealt with many problems and have fought hard to continue their ways of life. Many have made agreements with the US government that the government hasn't honored.

But all isn't lost. Art made by the native peoples of the Southwest has become very popular and received much praise. People from around the world treasure their crafts. This raises awareness about the importance of keeping these cultures alive. With new respect for these traditional ways of life, the future looks brighter.

Many native groups living in the Southwest today live on reservations. This map shows some of the largest native lands in Arizona.

Navajo Nation

Hopi

Hopi

Hualapai

Hualapai

Hopi

ARIZONA

TELL ME MORE

There are many historic places people can visit to learn more about the native peoples of the Southwest, including Mesa Verde National Park in Colorado and Pueblo Grande Ruin in Arizona.

Fort Apache

San Carlos

Tohono O'odham Nation

Tohono O'odham Nation

Tohono O'odham Nation

GLOSSARY

ancestral: having to do with ancestors, or people who lived before others in a family

arid: a very dry area that gets almost no rain

ceremony: an event to honor or celebrate something

council: a group of people who meet to discuss important issues

culture: the beliefs and ways of life of a group of people

descendant: someone who comes after another in a family

design: the pattern or shape of something

jewelry: pieces of metal, often holding gems, worn on the body

permanent: meant to last a long time

religion: a belief in and way of honoring a god or gods

tradition: long-practiced ways of life

universe: the whole world, space, and things people experience

weaving: the act or system of making cloth by crossing pieces of yarn or thread over and over

For More INFORMATION

Books

Krasner, Barbara. *Native Nations of the Southwest.* Mankato, MN: Child's World, 2015.

Sonneborn, Liz. *The American Indian Experience.* Minneapolis, MN: Twenty-First Century Books, 2011.

Websites

National Museum of the American Indian
nmai.si.edu
Learn much more about the many native peoples of North America.

National Park Service: Mesa Verde
nps.gov/meve/
Plan a trip to a site where ancestors of the Pueblo Indians lived.

Textiles of the North American Southwest
smithsonianeducation.org/idealabs/textiles/english/gallery/
See pictures of beautiful woven cloths made by native peoples of the Southwest.

Publisher's note to educators and parents: Our editors have carefully reviewed these websites to ensure that they are suitable for students. Many websites change frequently, however, and we cannot guarantee that a site's future contents will continue to meet our high standards of quality and educational value. Be advised that students should be closely supervised whenever they access the Internet.

INDEX

Ancestral Pueblo 8, 9, 10, 11, 16, 18
Apache 10, 11, 16, 18, 24, 25, 26, 27
bands 12
Cochise Culture 8
councils 12, 13
crops 8, 11, 14
families 12, 20
Geronimo 26, 27
Hohokam 8
homes 8, 9, 16, 17
Hopi 13, 18, 22, 23
hunting and gathering 8
jewelry 18, 19
kachina 22, 23
kiva 21
Mesa Verde National Park 4, 29
Mogollon 8
Navajo 16
pots 18
Pueblo 9, 13, 18, 20, 22, 24
pueblo 20, 21
religion 10, 14, 21, 22
reservations 27, 29
traditions 10, 11, 18, 22, 28
tribe 12
weaving 18
Zuni 13, 14, 15, 18, 19, 20